MARRIAGE HEAT

7 Secrets Every Married Couple Should Know On How To Fix Intimacy Problems, Spice Up Marriage & Be Happy Forever

LUCY LOVE

ISBN: 9781520357058

TEXT COPYRIGHT © [LUCY LOVE]

TABLE OF CONTENT

INTRODUCTION

Thank you and congratulation for purchasing the book *"Marriage Heat: 7 Secrets Every Married Couple Should Know On How To Fix Intimacy Problems, Spice Up Marriage & Be Happy Forever"*.

This POWERFUL book is written for any couple, whether newly married or has been in the marriage for a long while now; those who feel that their life has been going through tough times just because of their deteriorating marriage relationship.

After the first few years of wedded bliss comes and goes, many couples struggle to find ways to keep their marriage exciting. They don't know how to maintain the spark alive when they're dealing with stressful bills or trying to meet their kids' needs, or when both husbands and wives are so busy and stressed with their work, etc. As a result, heat and connection are lacking in their relationship. They tend to have no time for their spouse and children, particularly sexual matters between spouses is not as sweet as it used to be when they were newly wed couples. Therefore, it's likely to lead them to suffer from unhappy marriage/ broken marriage and even getting divorced

Marriage reveals and exposes who we really are. That's because when we say "I do," we enter a covenant relationship with our marriage partner. In business, partners seal their relationship with a contract, enforceable by law. Marriage can often be like a fence post. Before you witness signs of wear and tear above ground, the foundation of a relationship can be rotting away. That's is the reason we should ensure our marriages are made of heartwood—that they have the essential components to remain strong amid the stress and strain of modern life.

Did you know that marital success does not just happen? It is a direct product of the time and effort we put in it. It's just like a bank, whatever you put in like a savings or investment; you get back with a little profit. This is the same as your marriage or relationship. Whatever you put in, you get back with a little profit and a lot of couples don't understand this.

This book will examine the dos and don'ts in every marriage and how to build the glue that will keep you happy with each other for decades. I promise this eBook will be extremely powerful and you'll feel relieved to read it. Enjoy reading.

CHAPTER 1: TRUTH REVEALED: MARRIAGE IS NOT A BED OF ROSES - MY STORY

It has taken me fifteen years to write this book. I thought I needed a perfect marriage in order to speak to other women about improving theirs. I've realized I will never reach that goal, so I'm writing this book from my heart. I'm writing as someone who sometimes struggles with her feelings for her husband. There have been times I haven't felt much love for him; there have been times I've even wondered if I liked him. I'm speaking as someone who has come to the edge of divorce, but stayed—even though I didn't feel like it. I stayed believing that if I did the right thing, God would renew my love. Through my struggles, I've learned a thing or two, and I want to share them with you, not as an expert, but as a friend. I am imperfect, just as I suspect you are. I hope our hearts will touch at the point of our imperfections. And because of that, you'll be encouraged.

I was married in Houston, a state in the U.S. The church was filled with my friends, my relatives, and people of the community who felt like family because I'd known them all my life. The organist played the opening chords of the "Wedding March." I took my father's arm. The stiffness around his mouth was the only sign of the struggle he was having at giving me away to a man he hardly knew. We slowly walked down the aisle together, he was tall and proud, and I was frightened and excited, toward my beginning and his ending.

Richard looked pale. It was hard to tell if it was from the flu he'd had the week before or from the commitment he was about to make. We exchanged our vows. They were simple words that pledged our love through better or worse, richer or poorer, in sickness and in health.

If I'd been honest that day I would have said something like this: *"Richard, you've made me feel beautiful, feminine, smart, and funny. You're the first person who truly accepted me for who I am. We can talk about anything. The hours we've spent together have been pure joy. I feel fulfilled and complete. I've never experienced such happiness. And Richard, I expect you to make me feel this way for the rest of my life."*

Six months later, I sat in a small apartment in New York, which my parents referred to as a closet, and wondered what I'd done. All my friends were in Houston, and Richard, who only a few months before couldn't live without me, was too busy at his new job to talk to me on the phone. All I had was a black-and-white TV to keep me company. The man whom I couldn't wait to spend the rest of my life with now seemed distracted and uninterested. The fun-loving college student who took me to parties and movies and on sleigh rides suddenly had all these errands to run and chores to do. He measured the success of his days by how many things he marked off his to-do list. Resentment and dissatisfaction began growing in my heart.

Instead of dealing with it, I buried it. I never felt that I had a right to complain, and I surely didn't want to start a fight or hurt my husband's feelings. I chose another path. I moved back to college and obtained my degree. Tensions eased as I developed my own career, and we began to make plans for our future.

Six years later, we had a baby, a home, and two careers. We went to church every Sunday, participated in Bible studies and evangelism programs, planted flowers in the garden beds, and put on a smile for everyone who walked through our door.

We had it all when observed from the outside. Even if you had sat at our kitchen table, you would not have identified anything was amiss.

Then Richard found himself unemployed. I was frightened; he withdrew even farther. We became strangers sitting across the table from each other, and we were angry. We couldn't talk about anything without losing our tempers or getting our feelings hurt. I wanted Richard to fix what was wrong. But the more I yelled, the more he withdrew until neither of us wanted much to do with the other. We had no intimacy and whenever Richard made love to me, I had no true feelings. It was like making love to a log. We shared the same bed and even had another baby.

Two babies, a marriage that was failing, and we were Christians. A pastor told me it was a spiritual problem. Get right with God, then everything would be okay. I prayed, but it seemed as though God wasn't listening. I dreaded Sunday mornings.

I hated putting on that phony smile that said to the world everything was okay when everything wasn't okay. I withdrew from all of my church activities, avoided my friends, and started overreacting. I felt ashamed. I commenced playing with the idea of getting a divorce. Living alone had to be more honest than living this lie.

If you are where I was then, I have some good news. Divorce wasn't the answer. I found another way, and I want to share it with you. Through the chapters of this book, you'll discover a way back to the love that was once yours. Your marriage doesn't have to end. This can be the beginning of learning about yourself and rediscovering the man you married. It also can be a time to begin a lifetime of happiness, not because you have all the wonderful feelings that first love offers, but because you've seen your husband at his worst, he's seen you at yours, you've accepted who you are, and you want to remain married. It's a mature love; one made of steel because it has been tested.

In reclaiming my marriage, here are some of my actions:

* I decided to listen and pay attention. Settling arguments, decision making, and appeasing anger between spouses in marriage require listening. I learned the art of listening which has helped me iron out things easily.

* I decided to manage my finances well. Since I was in a good career, I had money to move me around. I had to divert away from luxuries and debts without the knowledge of my husband. Troubled finances between married couples will often result in squabbles and sad to say divorce can be looming on the way. I had to avoid this.

* Taking care of my children. I had to keep my kids clean and provide them with good food and nutrition. As much as I felt that parenthood is a matter of shared responsibility, I gave it an extra care to ensure that kids are clean, healthy, and well-taught. This was aimed at pleasing my husband who would later see a good homemaker in me.

* I had to limit jealousy. There are some jealousy levels that are flattering to a woman or man but it can also culminate into a habit that is very annoying. I decided to trust my husband in most of the occasions. I still do keep my jealousy levels to the admirable extent.

* Lovemaking is essential to a marriage. I had to make my husband enjoy the lovemaking. I had to do away with the olden history where men were believed to be the ones to initiate the act of lovemaking. I started making

him feel wanted. I went out of my way to be initiating the act. What else could I have opted for other than making him pleased in bed by incorporating variety and asking him what he likes.

* An attractive woman makes her husband happy. I had to make myself pleasing and attractive for my husband. The fact that we are married does not mean that I quit making myself beautiful to my husband.

* Marriage is all about commitment. Being loyal to him and keeping the promise has indeed been a good requisite of a happy marriage. I usually support my husband in times when he experiences bad days at work, since he got a new one after being retrenched from the first one.

* We are all human beings. Men admire to be appreciated as much as women do. I love to be appreciated and that is why I always appreciate my husband. I have cultivated the habit of appreciating the things that my husband does for me, our family and our marriage at large. He has weaknesses but I don't pick on them nor do I find faults to always scold at him. Appreciating him has made him reciprocate it with more good deeds and our marriage is very effective.

***

CHAPTER 2: THE TOP 10 REASONS PREVENT PEOPLE FROM KEEPING THEIR MARRIAGE EXCITING AFTER THE FIRST FEW YEARS OF WEDDED BLISS

Often, couples can't even pinpoint the exact reason as to why their marriage crumbled. There are endless things that could have gone wrong in a relationship. Just like a mechanic has to first detect the exact problem in a car in order to repair it, you too have to know the difficulties your marriage faces to salvage it.

No married couple could ever attest that their marriage is one that never encountered issues. There will always be problems in a marriage, few bumps along the road that couples must go through together. The success or failure of a married relationship will depend on the willingness and keenness of couples in undergoing marriage trials. Couples have better chances of going past these issues successfully by recognizing in advance what these problems might be.

Lots of marriages are collapsing today obviously due to problems encountered in the marriage. While it is important to find a means of resolving those problems, I believe it is even more important to know the causes of the problems and devise a way out of them. Below are some of the commonly encountered issues that spouses must know how to deal with.

1. Taking Your Spouse For Granted

Many marriages have been broken today because either one of the partners is not according enough priority to the other. As human beings, we feel fulfilled when our loved ones show us care, love, and appreciation. That is what your husband or wife expects from you at all times, no matter how little they have done, always show them how much you appreciate. Remember also that your husband or wife is your soul mate, hence they should be carried along in all your decision-making processes. Be it business, family, relationships etc. They should be allowed to be part of the decision that concerns your life interests.

2. Communication Problems

Every setback in marriage roots from poor communication. A person in a relationship may be busy and preoccupied with other things such as hobbies, pastime, gadgets and more. So as not to set aside communication, be sure that you and your spouse will set a schedule when you will be together to discuss things; without any form of distractions such as ringing cell phones and pestering kids. Suppose you have come to appoint when you communicate with one another with raised voices, it will be best to speak in a public place where you will be self-conscious about your voice tone. When one spouse is talking, the other should listen and not interrupt; instead, should wait for his/her chance to speak. When you listen, you must focus and show signs that you are listening such as nodding in agreement.

3. Conflicts

Conflict is part and parcel of any marriage. Conflicts are brought about by such issues as unpleasant comments or actions from a spouse that hurts the other spouse. Conflicts are unpleasant and bring about unhappiness. Factors that trigger conflicts may include rebuff, criticism, anger, dissatisfaction and unreasonable demands.

4. Technology Interference

Technology has played as a marriage distractor among some couples. Many couples spend a good chunk of their time online, on social media platforms, online dating and chat rooms. They provide less concentration and attention to their partners. For those in the corporate world, they spent most of their time on laptops trying to beat deadlines after office hours. This is leading to reduce intimacy.

5. Lacking trust

Not believing in your spouse has an 80% chance of causing a serious problem in your marriage. Imagine a scenario where you do not trust in the ability of your partner to remain faithful to you, imagine another instance where you believe they lie to you always? What do you consider will become of the marriage? The best way out of this marriage problem is to develop a very strong level of confidence in your spouse, it may take some time, but it's a very easy thing to do.

6. Sex And Intimacy Problems

Intimacy and sex are important elements of marriage. They help the relationship stay healthy. To give up on sex is something that couples should not resort to; as it is through sex that spouses are able to connect with one another physically, mentally and emotionally. If your schedules hardly give you time to make love, then all you need is to plan and create an appointment. This will even make you anticipate for that time and day when you are finally going to make love to each other. Create a list of things that turn each other on and use this list to make intercourse more pleasurable. If the issue has gone beyond repairable on your own, seek professional help from a sex therapist.

A sexless marriage is often a clear sign of a troubled relationship. Most people would be surprised however to learn that as many as 18% of married couples live in a sexless marriage, that is they have sex less than 10 times a year. It's also a myth to suggest that sexual passion declines with age. Sometimes couples that were in sexless relationships will rekindle their passion as they get older.

The reasons for a declining sex life are complicated but most commonly they arise from the stresses of daily life. Financial worries, work stresses, and health problems figure highly in this constellation of problems. This forms a backdrop of stress that builds up over time. What then follows is a two-way exchange that fractures emotional intimacy and which then carries over into the bedroom.

It's not always accurate to generalize but often women in relationships feel a stronger need to express their emotions than men do. A man who feels stressed will perhaps feel that he is being blamed for the difficult circumstances and will tend to close himself off. This denies a woman an avenue to express her frustrations and she will bottle them up. Unable to express herself and feeling that she is not being listened to, she will start to resent her husband.

If this kind of stresses persist a couple can start to drift apart and this will carry over into the bedroom. Emotional intimacy constitutes a large part of physical intimacy in a marriage.

Most people assume that men are driven more by physical desire but when emotional intimacy breaks down in a marriage it may be either partner who no longer wants to be intimate. Often there is an imbalance where one partner is rejected by the other. The feeling of rejection further escalates the tension in the marriage.

7. Financial Stress/Monetary Tension

Money is also a common cause of misunderstandings and arguments between spouses. Financial issues may begin even before you exchange wedding vows (from the wedding expenses). These are problems that must be taken care of with open mind and should be discussed seriously.

Money creates problems in the marriage, where couples are unable to adapt to other expenses and saving habits. Here are the reasons why the money can cause havoc on the marriage and lead to separation.

Lack of money: Some people marry young. They are not yet well established professionally. Therefore, do not earn enough. It may not be able to satisfy their materialistic ambitions. This can make people feel incompetent. This feeling of inadequacy can do to attack their spouses.

Debt: Loans and credit card debt that continues to add up to lead to anxiety about the future security of the family. Spouses are often unable to enjoy the company of others and appreciate the qualities of the other when they are in the troubled state of mind.

Refusing to compromise: the arguments of money arise when one partner refuses to agree on money matters. Each person has their own personality separate from the money. They have their own spending, saving, borrowing, loan or donation habits. For a marriage to work both parties must adjust and adapt to the personality of the money from each other. Sometimes, your personality can make money your spouse uncertain. Here you ready to change your money habits so that your partner does not feel threatened.

Be economically dominant and aggressive: Sometimes one partner tries to maintain absolute control over every dollar. When money is used to indicate a dominant position in a marriage relationship, creates resentment and anger.

Having too much financial pressure on a partner: Sometimes a business partner is responsible for meeting all financial needs of the family. He / she must earn enough for a month, and year after year to pay the electricity bill for the children going to school and university fees, to meet debt service obligations, to buy new furniture, and meet other requirements. This puts too much financial pressure on the spouse. I stress this because the partner is not for him / her to act grumpy and start petty disputes.

Children: A partner may start spoiling financial and destroy their children by buying them expensive toys and other gifts too often. The other partner can argue with that. In addition, one partner should pay child support to keep children from a previous marriage or relationship. The new spouse may not like that because it reduces the couple's monthly disposable income.

8. Married To The Wrong Person

Many marriages have been destroyed today because couples have the perception that they have married the wrong person. To be frank with you, this is not true when you consider the passion that got you hooked when you first met. Perception problem is a thing of the mind and needs to be dealt with from the mind. Harboring this kind of mindset is a very dangerous factor in your marriage because it tends to give you a force negative alert about your spouse, hence leading to the rise of problems in your marriage.

9. Lack Of Self Discipline

These marriage problems that I'm about to talk about can potentially make your spouse leave you. They are that serious. They revolve around the woman having no self-discipline and thus making her man feel like he can choose someone better to share his life with. It may be a scary thought, but if you're too relaxed with how you go about your marriage, these problems can be potentially very devastating. Self-discipline might be difficult but if your marriage is on the line, would you exercise more control over yourself?

1. Responding Negatively

When you respond negatively to your man, whether it be saying something to respond to something that he told you or making a comment about something related to him, this can do more harm than good.

You have to realize that a lot of the problems that make men want to leave you are a combined result of all the years of you chipping away at the marriage by not holding your tongue and thinking about what you say before you speak.

2. Letting Yourself Go

As much as you may want to stay young forever, it's easy to let yourself go once you get married. A lot of women simply get comfortable being wives and don't put in the effort anymore to impress their man.

Don't get me wrong, men do love you the way you are, but this doesn't mean that you can simply relax and not try anymore. If you try, they will try. If you all try, you will appreciate each other more for putting in the effort.

3. Men Channel You

If you have no self-discipline, that makes men not want to try as hard either. Men always need one person who's looking out for the marriage at any given time. If you simply don't care, the marriage will slowly slide into oblivion.

It's sad when people simply don't put in the effort anymore and the marriage just dies out of neglect. It does take discipline to make the marriage work and ultimately the people who put the most effort in and don't succumb to temptation will be happiest in the long run.

10. Infidelity

The simple meaning of infidelity is cheating! If formally defined, it is actually a breach of the expectation of having an all exclusive emotional and physical relationship with a person. This means that you and only you can share the same bed and have physical intimacy with your partner and you will be the only person with whom your partner will be sharing all his or her fantasies and secrets and emotions. This holds true for every culture, every person in the world and this exists even in those with a completely different sexual orientation. Infidelity or cheating can be broadly classified as sexual/physical infidelity and emotional infidelity. This essentially means that infidelity is not just about having sex outside a fixed and permanent relationship. It has a broader coverage which includes disloyalty, lying, betrayal, and trust. If a partner gets involved in a sexual relationship or physical infidelity with someone else after marriage, it becomes sexual infidelity which is also known as an affair, adultery or philandering.

This classification implies that infidelity is not just about moving out of the boundaries of an existing and permanent relationship to have casual or serious sexual relationship with someone other than the existing partner. It will also mean emotional attachment in which the person cheating will get emotionally attached to someone else and share all the secrets and emotions with that person instead of sharing those with the existing partner. It will also mean that the person will divert his or her emotional resources like love, attention, care etc. towards the other person and not towards the existing partner. Thus, infidelity is not just a sexual relation with someone else.

Superiority complex is one reason which is the cause of cheating. One partner can think that he or she is superior to his or her partner in terms of physical appearance or intellectually. This can push a person to cross the boundaries of a relationship and cheat the partner.

Excitement and challenge are yet another cause. The unfaithful partner cheats not because he or she has any grudge against his or her partner. Infidelity comes out of the fact that the unfaithful person looks for some fun, excitement, and challenge out of the daily routine of life.

Infidelity may arise due to change in the equation of love. If a partner spends more time with work or if a partner gives more attention to a newborn baby, the other partner may just feel unattended and this can lead to infidelity!

There are many reasons which can cause infidelity and irrespective of the cause, the outcome causes immense pain and suffering to the person who is being cheated. The pain caused by physical infidelity hardly requires any explanation. It is simple! A person will never tolerate his or her partner getting involved in a physical relation with someone else but, if that happens, it will be painful for the person. What about the emotional aspect? Emotional infidelity will be inflicting the same level of pain because the person who is being cheated will be facing the following:

- He or she will be in persistent fear that his or her partner might get involved physically with someone else. This is never acceptable and the constant fear brings emotional trauma.

- The victim will know that his or her partner is sharing his or her fantasies, emotions and secrets with someone else. This brings immense sadness and pain which remains inexplicable within the linguistic barriers.

- The person will know that his or her partner is diverting his or her emotional resources like love, attention and care towards someone else. This sense of ignorance and lack of love is extremely painful because sharing these pains are not easy!

So, if it is emotional infidelity, the pain may be same as that of physical infidelity and sometimes excruciating. So, if you have caught hold of your partner involved in infidelity, you must try to save your relationship by taking proper steps before it is too late!

CHAPTER 3: 7 SECRETS EVERY MARRIED COUPLE SHOULD KNOW ON HOW TO FIX INTIMACY PROBLEMS, SPICE UP MARRIAGE & BE HAPPY FOREVER.

Is there ever a marriage where you don't have problems? Well isn't it more so that marriage and problems are something that seems to fit together, at times way too well. But you can work through them with help. Books, counselors, and many other options that can succeed in saving a marriage. Once your marriage has hit rock bottom, it is the time that you take things in your hands and begin doing things that can salvage the marriage. Before you think of saving the marriage you should first believe in yourself and think of it as a fact that you can save your marriage. Once you start believing that you can save the marriage, half the battle has been won.

Marriages may just last once it transcends the physical to the emotional or the soul if you want to call it that. Marriages start with physical intimacy and over time it goes deeper and emotional bonding takes place.

Even the most *tarnished* marriages can be saved if you take the right steps in solving the problems you are facing. Be it something little like lack of sex, or something big like cheating. Either problem can be worked out, with help.

Maybe you're not the type that likes to announce to the world that you are having problems in your marriage. However, there are certain points where you may have to seek outside help. See, not all problems you come across are going to be fixed by just you and your spouse.

When you first got married to your spouse there were things about them that you felt you needed to have in your life. Focus again on those bright spots in your relationship; think of the good times. Work to get back to those feelings you had at the beginning.

Marriage and problems may seem like the same thing at times, but they really aren't. A marriage can be happy, and should be happy. However, it will take a working commitment from you and your spouse. You must be willing to give it all to be together.

However, in the same sense there will be a point you may come up against. The point where you just decide that you've tried everything, but it's not going to work anymore. People do grow apart for no other reason than they just get older. It happens, and may be the same in your case. Don't feel bad about the dissolution of your marriage if you've tried hard enough. Marital strife claims many victims each year.

Secret 1: Maintain Strong And Effective Communication

"Any problem, big or small, within a family, always seems to start with bad communication. Someone isn't listening." -- Emma Thompson

No matter how happy your marriage might seem to be, you will always have communication problems since we know that marriage is a process, not a destination. If something is bothering you or some behavior of your spouse is unacceptable to you, come out in open and speak about it. Your partner is never going to be aware of your deep-rooted fears and worries unless you voice them. For a healthy relationship, you need to learn to communicate effectively. So rather than be unprepared, here are 5 ways you can conquer communication problems in a marriage.

1. Know Your Spouse

Men and women approach relationships differently. A spouse might see the other as childish, annoying or overreacting. But the truth is that you just need to understand how both of you look at love issues. Communication problems are not about who is right or wrong. Build an understanding from how your spouse approaches love and marriage.

2. Be A Good Listener

What worsens communication problems even further is when spouses consider themselves to be wise enough to know what the other partner is thinking. When you interrupt before your spouse says something it can be very frustrating. Even if you have an idea of what is going to be said, hear your partner out. You will salvage the problems in your marriage if you do.

3. Stop Blaming

When one person has a problem, take it to be it is the relationship that has a problem and both of you should work it out. Never blame your partner for making you act wrongly or react badly. That is no excuse. When you say things like 'You make me sick' or 'You always bring the devil out of me', you are definitely taking it too far.

4. Keep Your Eyes On The Ball

When trying to communicate better in marriage, never bring up anything not related to improving your relationship. When you do this, you shift attention from what is important and worsen your marital situation in the process. Identify the problems and find solutions. Do not beat around the bush. Be focused and never petty.

5. Use Love Language

Your spouse is your partner in a relationship. Your spouse is a friend and a lover. Marriage is not a workplace so you are not a boss. Even when you have good points to make, it is important that you make them without criticism or condemnation.

Learn how to express yourself in love. Encourage your spouse to be a better individual. Let them know your thoughts when they do something you really like. Do not degrade them for anything. You affect the love and respect they have for you when you do this.

Communication is very important in marriage. They are effective and help solve issues in marriages. Give them a try today.

There, that doesn't sound too hard, does it? These techniques may be simple, but really do work to solve communication problems in relationships. Give them a try and rekindle your marriage.

Secret 2: Develop Positive Attitude - Give Your Partner A Priority

1. Positive Attitude: Note that marriage life is delicate, your relationship with your spouse may weaken at times, so a positive attitude is very crucial for ensuring that you can get through hard times, spice up your marriage, make it become stronger and happier. A positive attitude can also help you find more enjoyment and fulfillment in life, make your marriage always fresh and new. Try to avoid conflicts and arguments, pay more attention to optimism rather than pessimism in your relationship, start your conversations with positive thoughts, appreciate your partner's good qualities, be joyful, kind, respectful and give more smiles to each other, get rid of bad habits and revert them into good ones. Choose to think in positive ways, find solutions to solve problems together – trust your partner more, be kind and open with them, try to understand and meet their daily needs.

2. Give your partner a priority: As human beings, we feel contented when our spouses show us appreciation, care, and love. That is what your better half expects from you at all times. It does not matter however little effort they have put in, always display to them how much you appreciate. Remember also that your husband or wife is your soul mate, hence they should be carried along in all your decision-making processes. Be it business, family, relationships etc. They should be allowed to be part of the decision that concerns your life interests.

Being considerate, kind, loving and understanding to your partner. Let your spouse know that how much you respect and appreciate them. Let them know that you are very happy and appreciate every little thing they do every day for family like doing the cooking, washing, tidying up the bed etc. In return, you can do things that make your partner happy and appreciate you as well, e.g you wrote a love letter note thanking them for all of the things they have done for you, bring them a drink when they arrive home after work, give them a kiss or a hug, support your partner when they are occupied with tons of things like cooking, doing household chores, etc. Do apology when you do something wrong you think that hurt them, be considerate of their feelings, understand what they think about and what they want. Always be a good listener, be honest and thankful to your partner.

Secret 3: Arousing Your Wife's Sex Drive As A Man

If your marriage is on the rocks, just get back in the driver's seat and wake up your wife's sex drive. Take a leadership role and saving your marriage will be easier than you anticipated.

Adjust most of your negative thoughts into positive ones. If you master your mind, you will master your life and in turn, become the master of your relationship. You can change your habits, behaviors, activities, beliefs and ideas and enjoy the passionate rock-solid marriage or relationship you deserve.

Can you change to ensure that you save your marriage? And not only save it but to also grow to be the master of your relationship and fill it with love, romance, happiness with the added benefit - lots of great sex in fullness.

Be the leader in your marriage. When a woman is being lead by a charismatic, fun, loving leader she will do anything to make him happy. You see instinctively leadership is everything to a woman's sex drive. I know that thought is opposite to what you've been taught. You have been brought up to believe that men and women should be totally equal. In business and society, that is absolutely true. But in your marriage someone has to be the leader and that someone must be you, the man.

Return to the caveman's hunter mode by rebooting your brain. Return to the driver's seat. Reawaken the leader you once were so that your wife's sex drive will sense that you are a great leader and her attraction for you will fly through the roof. She will love and adore you unconditionally and you yourself will grow stronger and sexier than you have ever been.

And why is that you may well ask? Well, our sexuality is still very much governed by our Stone Age genetics where a male's sex drive and hunting skills had to be strong enough to ensure the survival of the human species. If you talk in reproductive terms men are simply sperm donors and providers, and women are programmed as the child bearers and nurturers. Cavemen were leaders, and that is what you need to be as well.

Sex drive is based on both biological, and psychological characteristics. The biological arm includes hormones, the nervous system, the brain and physical well-being. Actually, the brain is the biggest sex organ of all. Sex drive has its origins in the limbic system and the hypothalamus, which are the most primitive parts of the brain.

The psychological level is related to our feelings and thoughts; lifestyle and the environment; and on the quality of the relationship. It is controlled by the desire centers in the brain which control sexual desire and arousal.

These desire centers are controlled by hormones. The male hormone testosterone has a particularly important role. The desire centers send "sex currents" which control sex drive. This "sexual electricity" varies from day to day and from person to person so it is to be expected that everyone has different levels of desire and this will fluctuate from day to day depending on the circumstances. If your physical or emotional well-being are impaired then your sexual interest will possibly be reduced as well.

Sexual desire means feeling horny or having an interest in sexual activity. Sexual arousal means being turned on and physically ready to have sex. The higher your sex drive the easier arousal will be. Sexual desire emanates from love and trust in a close relationship and is a sign of good health and wellbeing. The factors which affect sex drive are:

- Neurological (the brain and nervous system)

- Hormonal (in particular testosterone)

- Personal wellbeing

- Physical wellbeing

- Relationship wellbeing

So, in conclusion, saving your marriage is easier than you think - the answer is to re-arouse your wife's sex drive by putting yourself back in the driver's seat. Arouse the leader in you and become the master of your relationship to save your marriage. The rest will follow.

Secret 4: Dealing With Infidelity

We just can't refuse the reality that unfaithfulness is very common in our times. A staggering number of couples, as much as 80% as reported by some gurus, will likely need to cope with infidelity. Even though we understand that the possibility of unfaithfulness is definitely high, it could be very painful when it happens to us.

An affair usually shakes the very foundation of a marriage and leads to many broken dreams and promises as well as leading to mistrust. In many cases, the betrayed spouse cannot move past these feelings of brokenness and hurt as well as mistrust and it may be very difficult for him or her to believe that the marriage stands a chance after an extramarital affair.

Of the many things that can destroy a marriage, infidelity is probably one of the biggest reasons for the disintegration of marriage. When a wedding occurs, the husband and wife promise before God and their friends and family to forsake all others and when a husband or wife does not keep this promise, the consequences can be devastating.

Infidelity can either be a sexual relationship with another man or woman outside marriage or it can be an emotional betrayal when a wife or husband is more connected emotionally to someone else outside the marriage. Many husbands and wives may identify emotional infidelity as more devastating to a marriage than sexual impropriety though both are detrimental to a marriage.

With the growth of online communities, chat rooms and various other social media such as Twitter, Facebook, and MySpace, it makes communicating with different people that much easier leading to emotional infidelity and cybersex that can impact a marriage negatively.

With the tough economic times, married couples are spending less time with each other as they try to make ends meet. This allows married couples to spend more time with other people in various workplaces and less time with spouses which is never good for any marriage and may lead to various opportunities for extramarital affairs.

Many other reasons may be used for infidelity but at the end of the day, they are simply excuses and the unfaithful partner willingly made a choice to betray the marriage vows and wreck havoc on his or her marriage. When cheating has happened, a relationship can be saved only if both parties are willing to do the work required without making any excuses or looking for scapegoats.

You can actually stop marriage infidelity by using the ideas discussed here. Simple one-night stands are improper but they are less distressing to your partner in comparison with emotional affairs. When you become too friendly with the opposite sex, emotional affairs might develop. It usually starts as a platonic association. The time you spend on maintaining pleasant connections outside of the marriage is the time that you could have spent with your spouse.

Honesty is required in any efforts to save a marriage and seeking marriage counseling or some other mediator may be wise. The first thing to determine is what was wrong with the marriage that led to the infidelity. There has to have been a reason that the wife or husband decided to break the marriage vows and carry on an extramarital affair knowing how hurtful it would be to the husband or wife if they found out about it. An extramarital affair may signify that the marriage has a brokenness that needs to be fixed if the marriage is to survive. If your husband or wife is simply a serial cheater, then saving the marriage is probably not in your best interests and you need to move on from him or her.

If you are the one that was betrayed by your spouse, you have to ask yourself if you are able to forgive your husband or wife who was unfaithful to you. Forgiving but not forgetting is not true forgiveness. You have to be willing to not bring up the issue over and over again and not play the blame game. This will only create bitterness and resentment that will lead the marriage nowhere. You have to be willing to put the hurt behind you and move forward otherwise there is no point in trying to save the marriage.

If you are struggling with feelings of unforgiveness, resentment, hurt, anger, etc, you may want to consider counseling for yourself if you are serious about doing your part in saving the marriage. Infidelity does not doom a marriage. If both parties have the willingness willing to move forward and heal the brokenness, the marriage can be saved. Both parties need to be honest with themselves and each other about whether they are willing to move forward.

Affairs usually lead to a breakdown of trust and in order to mend the marriage, the trust will need to be restored which may be difficult and the husband or wife who was unfaithful needs to be patient with the husband or wife who was betrayed.

Your actions during this period will have to line up with what you say. You have to be willing to say what you mean and mean what you say. If you say you are going to the movies, you need to be at the movies and so on. If he or she checks up on you, you need to know that this is a process of rebuilding trust.

Secret 5: Increasing Intimacy

Firstly, learn whether you lack intimacy within your marriage. Intimacy comes from sharing thoughts, sharing moments, sharing happiness, sharing problems and so on. If you or your spouse resorts to bury all your emotions inside and not share then it is going to create an emotional void with time. You have to be transparent as a glass with each other.

You must make it a norm to share each and everything with your mate. If you don't share you become preoccupied with your situation and begin to ignore your spouse. This attitude isolates each other and the situation becomes a one-way traffic where you start wondering what is going on while your spouse remains uncommunicative. The basic principle of marriage isn't being followed here which causes marriage complications.

It's extremely easy for partners to sense that something is amiss as soon as things go incorrect and you aren't being taken into consideration. This makes the other spouse isolated and hurts which can precipitate into your marriage getting down. To save your marriage, start sharing everything in your life so that you can build the foundation of your intimacy.

Here are some other useful ways help you to increase the intimacy level with your spouse:

1. Spend more time to take care of each other: Start spending some quality time with your mate to bring some intimacy inside your marriage. Spending time chasing a carrier or giving too much time to your kids are some of the reasons why most of the marriages fall by the wayside. Therefore, if you want to salvage your marriage find time to spend with your spouse.

Try scheduling around 15 to 20 minutes on a daily basis to have an uninterrupted conversation with your partner. Schedule a lengthy conversation on a weekly basis that may last for 1 or 1.5 hours. It will be a good practice if you plan at least one overnight after every two months just for the two of you. Always have at least two weekends on a yearly basis dedicated for the two of you.

Make your spouse laugh by telling them some jokes. You may go ahead to make them some drinks or foods when he/she feel tired. Make a sumptuous breakfast for your partner before he/she goes to work. During the weekends, ensure that you make them breakfast in bed. Believe me, you can never go wrong on this! I dare you to try as long as nothing is burnt and do not opt for cold cereal.

2. Surprise your spouse once in a while: You can surprise your partner with a little gift that he/she likes. It doesn't need to be expensive as long as you can bring a smile to them. For instance, you can buy your spouse flowers, chocolate or a small bottle of wine for no reason. You can also surprise your spouse by cooking him or her breakfast or dinner with food that they love, or you can tidy up the bedroom, replace old pillows with new ones, new colors match with your room and bed, or even lighting some candles in the bedroom at night.

3. Give a few compliments each other:

"When someone who loves and cares about me compliments me, I feel more glamorous than when the flashbulbs are going off on the red carpet." ~ Gabrielle Union

Do you find time to compliment your partner? Do you appreciate who they are? Do you make your spouse happy by your actions? It is the time you increased the number of compliments. Speak of nice or positive things about your special spouse when you are in front of other people. Positive things given to your spouse together with more compliments will increase their confidence in you and your marriage becomes happier each and every day.

4. Pick an exercise you both like and do it together: Do you remember your first instances of dating each other? Do you remember the crazy small things you did together that would make your hearts to glow with happiness? You used to run around the fields just like kids. You would walk around the streets holding each other. What a happy moment it was! Just go back to the same, pick an exercise you both like and do it together. There are some favorite exercises both of you like that are suitable for your age and time. You may choose to walk, swim, jog, play badminton or some other fascinating exercises. Exercise is extremely useful to bring you positive effects to both of you. You will improve your physical health and enhance the productivity in your sex life. It can help you relieve stress and improve your concentration in work and life.

5. Become a masseuse: Before retiring to bed, do you ever give each other a ten-minute massage? Become a masseuse. Most times you may get home from work feeling exhausted and your desire is to be left by yourself to rest. How wonderful is the feeling that you get when you take turns to massage one another's entire body.

6. Take a great chance of the morning time: The sun has risen. Did you realize it is yet another morning? Are you late for work? Did you just rush out of the bed into the bathroom and off to work? How many times have you repeated this? Oooh No! Style up and take some great moments of the morning time to spend with your spouse. When you wake up, spend a few minutes staying in bed a little longer, rolling over and putting yourself around your spouse's warm body. Give him or her a gentle kiss on the forehead.

7. Send a message once in a while: Write a flirtatious text message that will create anticipation, or one that will let your spouse know that you are thinking about them. Text him or her a message or email that says "I love you". Make your partner know that you are eagerly waiting for him or her at home and you would like to do something with him or her after work

8. Plan some special dates or weekends for you to get out together: Travel to some places you both have never been to. Taking vacations or weekend trips to places you both have never visited is a great way for both of you to enjoy activities together. Have you ever planned a scavenger hunt for your spouse? Plan for a romantic get-away and scatter hints in the house. Let your spouse struggle to collect the hints. Once they collect the clues and piece them together, let them be surprised to get a map of a nice place like Victoria Falls in Australia or a map of New England. Explain to them the plans and take off to the destination. Trust me, your partner will always remember that special trip.

9. Talk about new topics besides work, finance, kids: Try to read more books and find some interesting topics and bring them into your conversation. Watch movies and shows together and then analyze at the ending.

10. Change your hair and fashion style sometimes: Your spouse will really love to see you try something new or a new style that will make him or her smile. For example, you can change your old blouse, shirt or jacket for something new and attractive. You may also use a new lipstick to be more attractive. Shave your beard, wear new shoes, and throw away all the old ones.

11. Doing nice things once in a while: You may also place some life within your marriage by doing nice things sometimes, like taking a day off all of a sudden and go for a long drive. For example, you plan out a picnic to a beautiful beach, a park or somewhere else you have never been to. Such activities will spice up your marriage life and improve it to a large extent.

Therefore, building up intimacy in marriage not as a temporary measure but as an integral part of marriage for it to thrive.

Secret 6: Manage Your Finances

Whatever one's financial situation is must be disclosed and talk openly to the other person, including debts and income. Likewise, try to live within your family's financial capacity so that debts will not pile up. Save money if you can, no matter how small. When things are still on high heat, wait until the heat has already subsided so you can both discuss financial issues calmly. Discuss also about each other's plans or goals to extend financial help to each other's family like caring for elder parents. All financial goals (by an individual or as a couple or for the family), either long-term or short-term must be conferred with one another.

Secret 7: Allow Sex To Rule The Marriage

During the course of your day, you and your wife might talk about many things via the phone, email or texting messages. Topics between couples often revolve around money and bills, issues with the kids, aging parents or other family members and friends. Rarely do couples talk about the elephant in the room: the decrease in marriage sex. Relaxed sexual relations between a husband and wife keep the relationship healthy and bring a husband and wife closer together.

Be open in communication to ensure a happy and healthy marital relationship. If you can't chat openly with your wife about sex, this causes negative issues in the relationship, not just in your sex life.

Sex is very important in marriage because it allows couples to have fun together and create a strong emotional bond with each other. So if there is little or if there's no sex in marriage at all, then this could mean that there's a problem with your marriage which needs to be taken cared of. Read on as I share tips to help couples who are suffering from a sexless marriage.

1. Find Out The Reasons

There should be reasons why you and your spouse are no longer getting intimate, so you should find out what these reasons are in order to properly address the problem. Was it because you fight more often that you are no longer interested in having intimate moments with each other, or was it because of medical reasons? Whatever the reasons are, understanding and knowing the reasons behind your sexless marriage is the key to fixing this major problem in your marriage.

2. Do Not Quit On Your Relationship

Feelings of depression and of worthlessness are not uncommon symptoms to endure if you feel you are being held captive in a sexless marriage.

Be certain to work to mend these emotions if they play a part because they can only ruin the effort you can accomplish to fix a sexless marriage. There's always room for positive solutions to fix a sexless marriage just as long as you do not surrender and you try to stay optimistic.

3. There Is No Place For Blame

Issues will just become more severe if you start pointing the finger at your spouse. Rather than doing that, begin to understand why your other half has lost interest

Be aware of getting to the real reason otherwise, you'll never have the issue completely solved, and could wind up back to square one. Problems usually don't just pass, and the longer they are left unattended the more difficult it could become for them to be resolved.

Your relationship and intimacy issues will only worsen, while you are sitting around, waiting. Facing the difficulty and going back to discover the underlying problem that caused it is in your best interest.

4. Prioritize Sex

Sex has to be more than a belief; it has to be a value. Sex has to be a priority. You can believe that sex should be a part of marriage. But that belief can be underwritten with "if I feel like it" or "if he or she does what I want." However, when sex is a value of your marriage, both parties make it such a priority that they do what's necessary to protect that aspect of their relationship.

Challenge decisions that detract from intimacy. If your schedules are demanding, make an appointment for sex. Be flexible about the when and the where. It doesn't have to be a night thing; it can be a lunch thing. Anticipate challenges and plan for them. Build a supportive network or budget babysitter services into your financial plan. Make it priority to get into your partner's space.

Your marriage is worth the effort. When sex is really good, it strengthens the bond between a man and a woman. Keep that fire burning!

5. Prepare The Good Mood

Create the right mood and relaxing bedroom will add some spices to warm up your sex life. Add some candles or dim the lights to make the room become more romantic and extremely sensual. Turn off the phones, radio, televisions to avoid distractions. Play some jazz, sexy music to make your sexual intercourse more qualified.

6. Try New Things

Do not shy off from trying new things. The beauty of sexual intercourse lies in the secret of finding something new that makes you as a couple to reach the amazing orgasm. Try engaging in a little role playing scheme or practicing various sexual positions Spice up your sexual activities to ensure that you get the more exciting experience rather than getting used to the most traditional mode. You may decide to have longer foreplay as a way to make your sex life exciting. Make love in new places besides the bedroom. Make a date for the middle of the day, in the middle of the week. Get a room at a motel, dress drop dead sexy, wear lingerie in different colors and materials like leather, feather, silk, etc and enjoy an afternoon love making respite.

7. Make Sure That Your Health Isn't The Issue

Check to see if your partner is going through some kind of health problem in their life, that could have been the reason they have displayed less interested in sex together, and not because they have lost sexual appeal for you.

Consider this, as well as think about finding medical help as quickly as you can, after talking about it with your partner, so that you have the chance to heal your marital relationship that has become sexless. In many cases, however, a sexless marriage is caused by a much deeper problem in the relationship. You will be able to commence repairing your sexless marriage the sooner you acknowledge this and fix the underlying problem.

8. Do Not Be Too Uptight

Some of the women concentrate more on performing well in bed. On the vice versa, being too serious in bed does not guarantee that you will have superior sexual performance. Good sexual performance is a natural feat that grows with time as you gain more and more experience in sexual intercourse. Just let loose of yourself and drift into the act. Have the ability to control your sex drive.

As a man, it's important to take the lead in your marriage by talking to your wife about sex. Whatever you do, don't critique her or make her feel she doesn't measure up. This gesture will not work to improve your sex life. Try a dialogue that encourages your wife to speak about the things she would like to experience in your sexual relationship -- but be careful as to what you say as it is very easy to say the wrong thing. Reach out to your wife by showing your willingness to dialogue and try new things.

Words can be cheap, so find a way to show her you care. It's the little things that you do that stay with her -- helping out with the kitchen cleanup, giving her quiet time to read that magazine or book she wanted or finding a way to give her time away from the children.

Be your wife's best friend and be willing to listen to what she says. Many husbands don't take the time to listen to their wives because they think they have to do something to help "fix it" but all your wife wants is a friendly ear. This is the way that she works through her problems is by talking them out. What she's not interested in is hearing how you think she should fix it.

***

There has been a strange reversal from the pre-sexual revolution mantra of "no sex before marriage" to nowadays where the complaint is no sex, or rare sex, after marriage. Whether you are married or simply in a long-term relationship, being together for a long time tends to engender boredom or routine into your sex life. Common excuses are having children or they are too tired out after a day at work, or simply they are past all that. But I have found that many individuals have none of those reasons when they find themselves at a sexual lull.

Case Study - Ben and Jane. Ben had grown up always feeling at a loss around women, under confident and shy. He never found the knack of reading the signals women sent out and by and large, let them take the lead in relationships. Then along came Jane, and she blew his mind. He told me that from the moment he first laid eyes on her it was instant love. She made him feel so relaxed and comfortable he never felt any worries at taking the initiative in sex and for the first half-year, the sex was out of this world.

It wasn't just the sex that was great, but the whole relationship, so Ben had no qualms about asking Jane to marry him, even though they had only been together for a few months. He was deeply convinced she was the woman for him. Ben told me he couldn't pinpoint the exact time that he began to lose his sexual interest in Jane. It wasn't straight after they were married but it was pretty soon after.

A new and unwanted edge had crept into their relationship. Whereas in the beginning, the feeling of safety and security had given Ben the confidence to stick out, it now made him feel so comfortable he didn't want anything more, didn't feel the same passion anymore. As this went on Jane began to question why things had deteriorated but he hadn't the words so she soon fell into an acceptance that sex would be a "once a month" kind of thing. Ben, himself, took it for a fact that Jane would soon become pregnant and the presence of children would make sex a none issue.

Yet despite the apparent domestic harmony of their lives, they never fought or argued, Ben was shocked to find that Jane said she wanted to leave him.

She told him that while she still loved him, she just wasn't in love with him anymore. Ben knew in is heart the answer to why that was; it was the disappearance of the passion the spark that had previously been in their relationship. Ben then came to me, desperate to get back the spark and passion, but just so confused and scared of how to go about it.

The fear of losing Jane played on Ben's sexual performance. For the first time in his life, he began to experience premature ejaculation and impotence, all kind of problems he had never experienced before. He simply didn't know how to deal with these feelings, but what he did know is that it would make the task of keeping Jane all the harder. The tension-filled attempts at reigniting the spark only served to highlight their failing sexual connection. He tried exploring other avenues, talking to a psychologist, even taking medication, but nothing would provide the right solution and his confidence started to deteriorate to his pre-Jane days. He couldn't even find a way to initiate sex anymore.

What was the problem? This case was interesting; mostly men are thought of as sexual beings, it works or it doesn't, kind of mechanical in response. If it works fine, if it doesn't then off they go to the psychologist or therapist and "Bob's your uncle" it's sorted, like a mechanic fixing an engine. Even desire is thought of as automatic, we think men are always ready.

As we started to examine the dynamics of just what went wrong in their sexual relationship we made some interesting discoveries. Jane admitted that she hadn't always relished Ben's sexual advances even in the passionate beginnings of their time together. She shocked Ben by telling him that many times when they had been in the thrall of a passionate encounter she had actually been out of her mind thinking about other things and that Ben's intense need overwhelmed her completely. This set Ben thinking and allowed him to pinpoint when things started to take a turn for the worse. He remembered the feeling that Jane wasn't getting as much as she could from their comings together and that he needed to make more effort to make it as good for her as for him. He started having to put so much more effort into bringing her to climax and this was draining him, making him tired. He started to get the impression that Jane just wasn't on fire anymore. And unconsciously, his body had started to rebel, resisting the effort it took to have good sex and he came to see that no matter how much he still desired Jane, his drive had just gone away.

Sex of the Heart, Mind and Body. Strangely the root of most of our sexual guilt and indecision also contains the secret to our sexual liberation. You've got it, the Bible. I'm not saying that we should go back to the days of no sex before marriage, far from it. The Bible refers to sex as "knowing"; Adam "knew" Eve. Sex is more than a physical act, it is an awareness of the other. Every congress is an opportunity to become aware of yourself and of the person you are with. Every day we go about our lives being individual, we need to start to become aware of our Oneness. Unless we have the habit of using meditation we seldom stop and consider how we connect with those around us. In this modern world we don't simply cut ourselves off from other people but also our own self, our bodies, our emotions, just like Jane; she was perfectly able to carry out her day to day life, including sex with Ben, all the while, thinking of something completely different.

It is for this reason that routine sex is so harmful and, of course, why any sort of abusive sexual relationship is so deeply scarring. If the body is functioning on full throttle but the mind is several gears behind, or worse, in pain or afraid, then as an entity you are split in two. You are unable to experience yourself as a whole, to experience your Oneness and if you can't sort your own feelings out, how can you share in those of another?

So rather than rushing back in to rescue their sexual relationship, Ben and Jane would have been far better off had they started to become aware of one another again. Stopping to experience each other again. If you really want to touch someone else then you can't help but be connected to your own body - because how else can you really know who you are touching? Your body informs you. So reaching out to a lover to experience them and their body brings you straight back into experiencing yourself. This state of whole-body-mind awareness is how we should be all the time.

Finding the spark again. The simplest Tantra of all is to open your mind. How many times have you had sex whilst making a grocery list in your head? Or thinking about when you have to pick up the kids? Sex that is not experienced totally in the heart and the mind is not really an experience of sex at all. It is just another disembodied act that takes you further away from the way we are meant to operate. Real tantra is about being present and aware in every moment. In fact, doing the dishes can be an act of tantra if it is done with awareness - a single pointed focus on exactly what you are doing. Within this single pointed focus hides the deepest level of relaxation, focus, and creative potential. This is entering into the true Yin state, a state of receptivity and awareness and from this focus, your creative and spontaneous energies will flow naturally. There is no effort required. And we all know that the best sex is when you lose yourself in it and in the other person. Sharing this space with someone else is a sacred experience because you are totally open and totally receptive. This is when you merge with your partner. Your receptivity goes beyond your own body into theirs and you are experiencing your true nature.

CONCLUSION

Marriage is a wonderful manifestation of love and affection between two people. And although marriages are based on the strong foundations of love and commitment for one another, a marriage that is marked by traces of selfishness can lead to failure. While you cannot expect your partner to be perfect, it is very important that you also give utmost importance to their feelings and needs instead of just focusing on your own self. Always love and respect your partner if you want your marriage to end up a success.

Did we mention about health in marriage heat and happiness? Your marriage bliss grows when you decide to eat healthy foods that will make the two of you strong. Accept your partner, forgive them and always sleep healthy in each others' arms. Workouts are a great boost your self-esteem. Do something together that will always plant a smile on your faces like listening to your favorite songs, watching a movie together, spending time in a crocodile park, or having a bubble bath together. Marriage is a beautiful journey and if you learn to cherish the similarities and respect the difference, you can make every moment worthwhile.

Thank you again for downloading this book on *"Marriage Heat: 7 Secrets Every Married Couple Should Know On How To Fix Intimacy Problems, Spice Up Marriage & Be Happy Forever"* and reading all the way to the end. I'm extremely grateful.

If you know of anyone else who may benefit from the informative tips presented in this book, please help me inform them of this book. I would greatly appreciate it.

Finally, if you enjoyed this book and feel that it has added value to your life in any way, please take a couple of minutes to share your thoughts and post a REVIEW on Amazon. Your feedback will help me to continue to write the kind of Kindle books that helps you get results. Furthermore, if you write a simple REVIEW with positive words for this book on Amazon, you can help hundreds or perhaps thousands of other readers who may want to enhance their marriage life have a chance getting what they need. Like you, they worked hard for every penny they spend on books. With the information and recommendation you provide, they would be more likely to take action right away. We really look forward to reading your review.

Thanks again for your support and good luck!

If you enjoy my book, please write a positive review <u>HERE</u>

-- Lucy Love --

Check Out Other Books

Go here to check out other related books that might interest you:

Daughter of Strife: 7 Techniques On How To Win Back Your Stubborn Teenage Daughter

http://www.amazon.com/dp/B01HS5E3V6

Parenting Teens With Love And Logic: A Survival Guide To Overcoming The Barriers Of Adolescence About Dating, Sex And Substance Abuse

http://www.amazon.com/dp/B01JQUTNPM

The Shocking Truth About Sexual Blackmail: The Secrets Cyber Scammers Don't Want You To Know - The World's Best Advice On How To Deal With Sexual Blackmailers

http://www.amazon.com/dp/B01IO1615Y

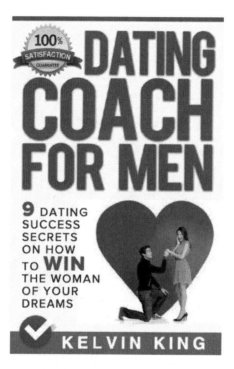

Dating Coach For Men: 9 Dating Success Secrets On How To Win
The Woman Of Your Dreams

http://www.amazon.com/dp/B01IOHIPNY

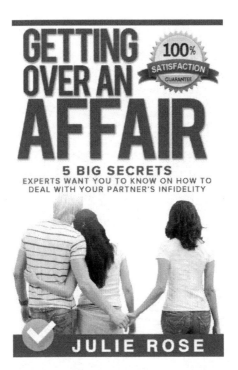

Getting Over An Affair: 5 Big Secrets Experts Want You To Know On How To Deal With Your Partner's Infidelity

http://www.amazon.com/dp/B01J7G5IVS

Productivity Secrets For Students: The Ultimate Guide To Improve
Your Mental Concentration, Kill Procrastination, Boost Memory And
Maximize Productivity In Study

http://www.amazon.com/dp/B01JS52UT6

Made in the USA
Columbia, SC
14 December 2021